Walking from Origins

poems by Mary Moore Easter

Heywood Press
Northfield, Minnesota
Copyright 1993

In Dakar I do not know Wolof
or how to find the Marchée Kermel.
I do not know
how to bargain the merchants down
to a reasonable price
for my sandals.
But some things I do know
and Orion is one of them
in a dark sky over whatever continent.
The three stars of his belt
shine down tonight
on my hotel.
His ebony face hovers.
He whispers
    As salaam aleikum
    Welcome to Africa
    Nak nga deff.

"Before it stopped raining in Senegal..."
he said, as we drove through the
dark streets, white buildings
old arcades, sleeping bundles
of people far from the green of the past.

"before it stopped..."
sand beds in the south stretch for minutes
puddle-dotted where the water used to rush,
lake-side rocks stranded in red sand.
Baobab forests sprout leafless appendages,
crooked black fingers that point to a dry sky
a desert wind, a red dust.

"Before it stopped raining in Senegal
things were so different..."
The ocean invades the rivers
and salt chokes the water lilies.

But the gardener at the Nema Kadiour
still dances the fire dance once a week,
leaving his hotel-issued overalls
and moving bare-chested to the head of the troupe.
Every move you make is still
everyone's open-eyed business.
The dancers still bare their breasts to remind you
of the children they will suckle.
And the drums send joy through the evening.

ATLANTIC PASSAGE

I.

Elaine said: Get there early so you can watch the theater of the dock. There's such theater as they load.

Elaine said: Get a private cabin with a tiled shower, a t.v. and fluffy white towels. You'll arrive refreshed in the morning.

Elaine said: Book it soon while the boat's still new and clean. Girl, you have to go.

So I booked an overnight passage from Dakar to Ziguinchor in my very own private cabin with a white-tiled shower and a t.v., and I got there early and Elaine was right. There is much theater on the dock as the cars back onto the boat with everybody directing, and the women with bunches of blue plastic jugs load them to bring back palm oil and palm wine. And the men stand around and pee on the nearest walls, and only one couple holds each other Western-style around the waist, and friends see them off.

Even though two groups of Muslims argued in the newspapers today about which night was the end of Ramadan because one side claimed the other was blind to moonlight, I spot the crescent above me and to the right. The deck sways slowly under the moon, riding the sea's deep memory with long practice. Merchant women pad themselves with money inside their printed drapery, and wave to the disappearing dock as we slide into the night above and below us.

There is much theater as a trickle of people find their way to the sudden quiet of first class cabins, more theater as a crowd locates their second class seats lined up in airplane rows with strangers holding the baby while Mama gets the bundles settled. But there is maximum theater in third class where every inch of the boat's floor is covered with batiked and shawled people eating out of tin tubs, sleeping, nursing babies, quieting the chickens who try to flap their way out of bound legs. Maximum theater as children peer out the portholes, stepping from mat to mat to get closer to the licking sea. Third class knows at a glance I don't belong to this village no matter how I drape my batik shawl and inquire *à quelle heure* the boat will arrive in Ziguinchor. Their wave of theater is so strong it sends me back to the confinement of my white-towelled cabin.

II.

But the night is for celebration, for release from a moon's cycle of restraint. The bar floods with music, high spirits and too many people wondering if I'm Senegalese or exactly what, made uncertain by my head wrap and request for *"une biere"*. The beer arrives hand over hand with "hello, Laydee, hello, Sistuh. Where are you from? Where are you going? Are you married, Laydee?" Exhausting to be the object of constant interest, eyes always on me. Not sex they want in this country, not my body but my soul.

The men crowd closer like at the ship's ticket window this morning, so many people handling my business with the ticket agent that I can't get a word in edgewise until I shout, *"Assez, mes amis, assez. Silence."* They don't seem offended in the least at this command for silence and press close to the window like they press now. The music escalates, tired children run circles around the tables after a late dinner. The whole room seems to pulsate, circle and press.

III.

In my cabin the tv is bound to its high shelf, a blank screen. I turn it on just in time to see the picture go to static, gray/black buzzing. We've lost contact with the shore. At the window, I can't see the rolling ocean in the dark and wonder how high the waves are. I hear someone walking in the hallway. I listen at the door. Or maybe they're on the deck outside my window. They must be drenched.

This colorless room is so different from the sights of Dakar, no pattern here, no activity, no music or laughter, no one bidding for my attention. The room creaks with peace and quiet while the ocean howls outside the windows. I lie on my shelf of bed, feel my liquids float on the sea within the boat of my body, heavy now in my head, now in my belly. My heart rocks, my blood rocks, my brain slides from side to side in my skull. I don't last long in solitary.

IV.

Back for another beer, I find the rolling boat has heightened the restaurant's frenzy. Music throbs with trumpets, two couples dance Western-style, out of time with each other, awkward in their embrace. A merchant woman dances alone on the sidelines, her front stuffed with thousand franc notes which move in a single block while her hips create a fugue of rhythms from the rear. The ticket agent from the morning appears, bottle in hand, and asks to see my ticket. Why? We are in the middle of the Atlantic. Surely every one is accounted for by now. He insists. I fumble in my purse not finding the little stub. He presses. He's the *"contrôle"* and must assure himself that all present have their proper tickets. I look down into his aggressive face, the insistence of the drunk in his eyes. Out of here. Too much noise again, too much hassle. I lurch my way back to my cabin for the third time, back to the spirits, the solitary rolling, the unseen waves and howl of wind.

V.

I bet third class is a sight to behold. Plenty of color and pattern down there. People crowded together on benches of wooden slats, huddled on the floor, rows of them. And the timbers creak and the boat rolls and we lie, packed tight like spoons, chained to an eternity of sickness, stench and darkness. Wait, wait. Time has given me the slip. No. Here, I'm here with the white towels and the tiled shower, not there. I'm here and only an hour ago the tv showed No Way Out dubbed in French.

No way out of this nightmare, this boat full of Africans leaving the African shore, passing Gorée somewhere in the night, "island of the cursed" they called it even before it was a slave port.

And the sea holds them all, their bones, flesh of the sick and dead thrown to sharks, limbs of the hopeless looking for a way out. The sea splashes them against my window, howls, rages, remembers every one of the millions who bang on the walls of my colorless cabin. There is not enough music in the bar to drown them out, not enough beer to float them away. There is too much music in the bar and too much beer to quiet them. I walk the night halls from haunted cabin to whirling bar, the rolling halls, listening to their cries, glimpsing their shapes thrown up on the windows, flitting from wave to wave. Some open their watery mouths as in a scream, some claw the air in a desperate dance. Sails snap in the wet wind. The century has slipped out from under me and I seek my footing on waves, on the same sea that bore them away forever, that sucked them down to singular escape, the sea that guards their souls and echoes their cries. I am walking, falling, reaching on water, on water, water.

ILE DE GOREE

Everything here knows how to wait.
Stone houses, stone walls
mortar eaten by time
lanes of beach sand.
My feet leave indentations
too shapeless to be called prints.
No cars, not one person
since I left the cafe at the dock.
Silence.
Brilliant bougainvillea curves down
to touch the rumpled desert sand.
Then a courtyard's open door
a glimpse of women braiding hair
a pump, washed clothes.
I pass like the low buzz of their radio,
scan the pinwheel of empty streets.
No body fills the hollows in the sand.

Except for electric wires overhead
I have travelled to the living past
barred windows, shuttered balconies
stripped bones.
I slip through without a trace.
The trees are too old to die.
Their roots reach down
through sand and rock.
They know a way to drink
the sea's salt water,
make orange flowers from it.
Everything here knows
how to survive.

IN FRONT OF THE HOUSE OF SLAVES: I

The spirits behind this door know my name. Such spirits waiting for me, their misery, our grief. I travelled all this way just to stand in their tracks. I reversed their journey, came east over the sea to put my feet in their foot prints, feel them cluster about me. And waiting in front of this door, I know they know my name. A tall Frenchman in the crowd has had his hair braided *à l'africaine*. He bellows laughter at his companion. He looks ridiculous with his slick white hair in tiny braids sticking out all over his head, each braid needing to be secured with a rubber band otherwise the weaving slides loose on its own. Not like the hold and cling of African hair. I don't like his braids, a joke for the benefit of his friends. I hold on to my insult at his tiny braids to keep from flying the tiny flag of me that wants to dance in honor of reunion. Don't fly your flag. You must not fly your dancing flag of welcome, or it'll be like the day in the Sweetbriar museum where the guide handed me a slave bracelet, a coiled silver snake dug up on the place. And my hand, touching it, slid inside that slave's hand, right inside her skin. We held hands across centuries, this unknown woman who wore this bracelet all the way from her home, battling the Middle Passage, fighting it to the end, to Virginia to work her life away, her bracelet buried in the earth without her arm in it, lost, thrown away, now sitting on the museum's mantle, now in my hand, my hand in hers.

And if I fly my dancing flag today what woman will come forward when they open the courtyard door exactly at three o'clock? What woman wearing her indigo cloth with white lines of palm leaves, will rush forward asking if I have seen the baby they tore from her breast, wanting to know if her brother is already in the ship, if the cries she heard at night were those of her husband. Of all of us who wait, I am the one she will ask in a strange language as if I understood about the lost baby, the shipbound brother, the weeping husband.

IN FRONT OF THE HOUSE OF SLAVES: II

Tight my jaw against the tourists' laughter
neckline tight, belt secure
shirttails in, lips drawn thin,
everything about me tight except
the flutter of indigo cloth
at the corner of my eye.
Nothing left to tuck in when I turn.
Still, it flits and wavers
tiny quivers inside my eye.
What is this flicker
waiting at the House of Slaves
that flaps in leaps and starts,
that agitates?
Clearer now the flash of fine white lines
ripple of palm leaf veins on blue
so deep and black:
this tiny me that wants to dodge
through crowds,
that jumps and flashes
before the scarred door;
a blue batik of me
that wants to bow low,
stamp the drums to life
the past so near at hand,
this tiny flag of me that wants to dance
in grief and fear and honor.

IN THE COURTYARD

      The door opens at three o'clock, big wood door grinds, and we are herded through the dim entry into the brilliance of the courtyard. Set on yellow sand, an astonishing house gleams pink stucco. Above, a trader's heaven looks down at us, ocean views, long elegant windows, high veranda. Below, a slave's hell of dark cells, doorways gaping like toothless mouths, sand floors. Between them the gracious curves of twin stairways. What architect of perversity made beauty for this spot? Beauty in the very bones of this house, the marrow evil. Beauty of form, evil of function, perfectly allied.
      The intimacy of this courtyard puts horror on a human scale. Small to house thousands, close. Down here on the ground, these square rooms with low ceilings and loose sand floors are too small for their huge history. In the room to my left, the woman who waits for me could call across the courtyard. She could easily distinguish her own baby's cry just beyond the stairs, her breasts engorge with milk at the sound. She could recognize the wail of her brother, familiar from dreams and nightmares since she was a child. She could call out in a whisper, be heard before they took her away.

      Ghosts of their cries
      whistle past my head
      shouts and whispers
      crisscross the courtyard
      hurled from open-mouthed doorways
      spit from between slit lips
      making dark tracks in the sun
      disturbing the sand into yellow dust.

Who guards the portals at the house of slaves
who weighs the men
who force feeds them
who separates the women
from the children
from the men
who slops the overflowing tubs
in the corners of the cells
who cooks the trader's breakfast
in the rooms above
who clears the table on the veranda
who washes milady's linens,
polishes the trader's floors
who listens to the cries at night
who smiles and serves and obeys
intimately acquainted with the price?

The jailer's son limps
on one whole foot
and one half foot.
He jangles the jailer's keys for play.

The jailer's son brings
the lunchtime fish and rice
in a big calabash.
He squats with his father
by the courtyard door.
They eat from the bowl
scooping right hands
to their mouths.
The jailer's eyes fall
to the half foot beside him.
He knew what to do.
He has no regrets
though he remembers
the screams of his son, the fever,
the visions they shared,
the healing at last.

Behind the big door
boys with whole feet
and whole arms
will be sucked away
but the jailer's son limps
so he can stay
to bring the lunch tub every day.

The French drift away. Alone, I stop in the doorway of the first square room, stand there eyes searching the walls, the loose sand on the floor. From the far corner, a few feet away, a wail like the imam's five a.m. prayer curls up out of the sand, spirals in white smoke toward the low ceiling, cracks at the high point and disperses into the moaning air. I stand pulling something in, pulling in the air they exhaled from their lungs, collecting scattered soundwaves, the faint click of beaded braids, the rattle of cowrie shells, the soft thud of leather-pouched magic against a thigh. The studded drums of my ears search for vibrations from centuries, for soft-tongued syllables, the blunted "t", the snap of whip, rattled chain, the soiled laughter of sexual bargain.

The ground under my feet knows something I must know. My eyes split into facets, look forward, back, sideways, reflect angles of time, penetrate walls, slip between stones and each grain of sand. I will myself to memorize footprints, the peel of the walls, the one window without bars. My hands palpate raw air, shape distant presence. My skin detects the passing of ephemera. Tentacles from my feet tangle in deep tree roots, suck them of old tears, spilled blood. I lean toward the distant voices behind me, chatter of past and present mingle.

In the second room:

Her name is already lost.
Around her strange languages
muffle the air,
tribes she does not know,
practices she has never seen.
Elbows braced, the corner at her back,
she listens for her name
from any room in any tongue.
Blind, mute, beyond the crush
and scent of bodies
every sense defaults
to her ears

which strain the air
for this one sound
her name
her name
the name of her people.

THE CONJURER

A conjurer stood here in a red robe.
She-lelele, sh!, she-lelele, she-lelele, shhhhhh.
She-lelele, sh!, she-lelele, she-lelele, shhhhhh.

The day they brought him
through the gates
the African guards fell back
to see him yoked in wood and chains.
They would not touch him.
The trader's manservant had to be called
to take the yoke from his neck
to shove him into the crowded cell,
"just another surly ragged soul."

She-lelele, sh!

The bodies parted as he stumbled in
made space around him
where there was no room.
His eyes blazed stillness
and his wrist shook rhythm
from the rattles of his bracelet.
She-lelele, sh!, she-lelele, she-lelele, shhhhh.

He never tired through day and night.
He did not open his lips
nor sit, nor sleep
as he blazed and rattled himself to purity.
The rhythm of his rattle
spread silence from cell to cell.
Cries stopped, moans dispersed,

the sick rose to their feet,
no one ate.

Two hundred years ago
a conjurer stood on this spot
in his red robe.
I leave space around him.
She-lelele, sh!

Here they weighed them, all sold by weight, boys fattened to a man's sixty kilos in this very room. The space swings with the balances of absent scales -- reels and swings. Paint peels here, too, layers of mud wall exposed, the jagged fit of island stones. I lick the swinging air for human salt, send my nose into corners like a hungry dog sure of all it will find there, the musk of human fear. A monster of insistent senses, my body will own this past.

A whisper away, small rooms on the sea, slits for windows called *"meutriers"* -- murderers. A narrow corridor of murderers, slits to hold guns trained on raiding ships. Windows called murderers instead of the traders. Murderers. A good word for this place.

* * * * * * * * * * * * * * * *

Dark to light. Light to dark. Dark to sea light. Sand gives way to black stones in the final passageway. Caged lamps flicker overhead. It was like this, bodies at my back, in front of me, a cortege in slow-time toward the sea, going into the dark, into the light of day, sent anytime their numbers would fill the boat. Enough feet on these stones to wear grooves in them, the dull chink of chain on shackles, the hush of dread anticipation. From this doorway on the sea no one ever came back, was ever heard from again. The rumor must have spread from the lame and rejected, the thin and sickly, those aged and unsold, that on Gorée was a doorway on the end of the world. If your brother entered, your sister was pushed, they would vanish into thin air, step into the unknown, breech space into another world, a different dimension. And in the distance boats waited.

I edge toward the doorway of no return, balance without touching the walls they touched, do not want to see what they saw leaving, do not want the dark square rooms full of home at my back. Black stones rim the sea, vomited from the passageway through the mouth of the door. Water. No end of it. No bottom.

Requests to the black stones:

Let me hear the rustle of escape.
Recount to me the first midnight swim
before the sharks learned where
to wait for thrashing human food.
Tell me the story of the ones
who swam all the way home
dragging themselves onto the shore
at dawn, lungs burst, legs spent
eyes rolling in their heads with freedom
and the final fatigue.

tell me of the foot that landed here
in haste, pushing off in a flying leap
to the rushing water.
Was it man or woman?
Did the diver pause mid-air
at the sea's uncertain depth,
the distance to the mainland?
Or rush headlong into any fate
bound to be better than the fattening room,
mouth pried open with metal, teeth broken,
food forced down the closed throat,
gagging body of resistance,
tongue choking on blood, teeth
and the food of bondage.

    I've flown twenty hours and taken a ferry so I can walk this hallway and stand at this door on the edge of the world. I look down at black rocks shiny with the slap of the sea, beer cans, rags, faded newspapers, debris of the twentieth century at my feet.

WALKING FROM ORIGINS

Go back to the moment
on the African coast,
the instant of change
a conjunction of time and place.

Freeze the picture
with the foot lifted
to step from earth to water,
from birthright to bondage
from a nation's "we" to an "I"
in lower case,
trampled in the scuffle of history.

In that instant the command was,
"Walk on water or die."
Some chose a death they devised,
sealed lips, shut eyes,
soul flown from the body.
Some seized an unguarded second
to leap en masse from the clutches
of destinies planned by others.
Those that did not choose death,
walked on water.
They walked with hands bound
and chains on their feet.
They walked lying in their own filth.
They walked through blindness and rot
they walked alone and with strangers
they walked with the whip on their backs
they walked with nothing under their feet
except water.
They walked on water.
And they keep on walking.

TO THE ANCESTOR SPIRITS

I came to tell you
something came after.
It was not just suffering
to no end, a finish in death,
a blank wall.

I came to tell you
something lived on and grew,
reached its arms out to circle the globe,
dug fingers into the rivers of the new world,
buried flakes of skin in the jungles
of the southern hemisphere,
fingernails in the rocks of coral islands,
dripped blood into deep wells of dry places.
Hair clippings blew like seeds
over northern plains.
Drops of sweat fell thick in planted acres.
And they sprouted.
All manner of cells grew their new fruit
from original seeds.

I am a fruited messenger
come to lay myself on your bones
so that you may know
something did come after.